Dinosaurs

# Triceratops

Daniel Nunn

# H www.heinemann.co.uk/library
Visit our website to find out more information about Heinemann Library books.

To order:
☎ Phone 44 (0) 1865 888066
Send a fax to 44 (0) 1865 314091
📄 Visit the Heinemann Bookshop at www.heinemann.co.uk/library to browse our
🖥 catalogue and order online.

First published in Great Britain by Heinemann Library, Halley Court, Jordan Hill, Oxford OX2 8EJ, part of Harcourt Education. Heinemann is a registered trademark of Harcourt Education Ltd.

Editorial: Daniel Nunn and Rachel Howells
Illustrations: James Field of Simon Girling and Associates
Design: Joanna Hinton-Malivoire
Picture research: Erica Newbery
Production: Duncan Gilbert

Printed and bound in China by South China Printing Co. Ltd.

10-digit ISBN  0 43118447 X
13-digit ISBN  978 0 4311 8447 0

11 10 09 08 07
10 9 8 7 6 5 4 3 2 1

**British Library Cataloguing in Publication Data**
Nunn, Daniel
Triceratops. – (Dinosaurs)
567.9'158
A full catalogue record for this book is available from the British Library.

**Acknowledgements**
The publishers would like to thank the following for permission to reproduce photographs: Alamy pp. 6, and 23 (Christian Darkin), 14 (Jeff Morgan), 19 (Phototake Inc.), 20 (JupiterMedia); Corbis pp. 7 (Gary W. Carter), 18 and 23 (Annie Griffiths Belt), 21 (Paul A. Souders), 22 (Louie Psihoyos), 22 (Philip Gould); Science Photo Library p. 12 (Christian Darkin).

Cover photograph of Triceratops reproduced with permission of Alamy/Christian Darkin.

Every effort has been made to contact copyright holders of any material reproduced in this book. Any omissions will be rectified in subsequent printings if notice is given to the publishers.

# Contents

The dinosaurs . . . . . . . . . . . . . . . . 4

Triceratops. . . . . . . . . . . . . . . . . . 8

How do we know?. . . . . . . . . . . . . .18

Fossil quiz . . . . . . . . . . . . . . . . . 22

Picture glossary . . . . . . . . . . . . . . 23

Index . . . . . . . . . . . . . . . . . . . . 24

Notes . . . . . . . . . . . . . . . . . . . . 24

# The dinosaurs

Dinosaurs were reptiles.

Dinosaurs lived long ago.

Triceratops was a dinosaur.
Triceratops lived long ago.

Today there are no Triceratops.

# Triceratops

Protoceratops

Some dinosaurs were small.

But Triceratops was big.

Triceratops had thick, strong legs.

Triceratops lived together
in herds.

Triceratops walked slowly most of the time.

But Triceratops could run
fast, too.

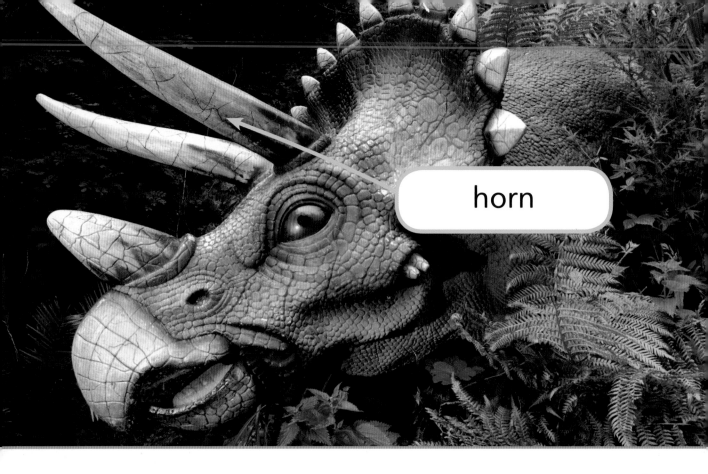

horn

Triceratops had three horns.

Triceratops used its horns to
fight other dinosaurs.

But Triceratops did not eat
other dinosaurs.

Triceratops ate bushes and plants.

# How do we know?

Scientists have found fossils
of Triceratops.

Fossils are the bones of animals which have turned to rock.

fossil

Fossils show us the outline
of the dinosaur.

Fossils tell us what Triceratops was like.

# Fossil quiz

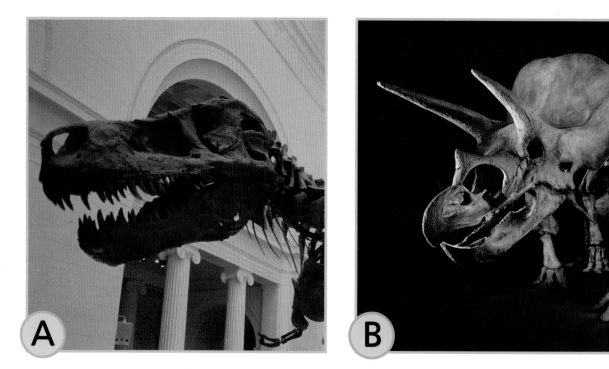

A

B

One of these fossils was Triceratops.
Can you tell which one? Turn to page
24 to find out the answer.

# Picture glossary

 **dinosaur** a reptile who lived millions of years ago

 **fossil** part of a dead plant or animal that has become hard like rock

 **horn** a hard pointed growth on the heads of some animals

 **reptile** a cold-blooded animal

# Index

fossils  18, 19, 20, 21, 22    reptile  4

herd  11                          scientists  18

**Answer to question on page 22**
Fossil B was Triceratops.
Fossil A was Tyrannosaurus rex.


**Note to Parents and Teachers**
**Before reading**
Talk to the children about dinosaurs. Do they know the names of any dinosaurs? What features did they have e.g. long neck, bony plates, sharp teeth? Has anyone seen a dinosaur fossil or model in a museum?

**After reading**
- Measuring in the playground
  Tell the children that some dinosaurs were larger than the classroom. Give them a ball of wool to measure Triceratops (11 metres), Diplodocus (28 metres), Brachiosaurus (25 metres). Staple the lengths of wool to the classroom walls.
- Make a head band for each child. Ask them to draw the head of a dinosaur onto card and cut it out. Tell them to decorate the headband and then staple the dinosaur head onto the band.
- Read a fiction book to the children e.g. *Harry and the Bucket Full of Dinosaurs* by Ian Whybrow (Puffin).

# Titles in the *Dinosaurs* series include:

Hardback     978-0431184500

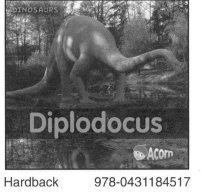

Hardback     978-0431184517

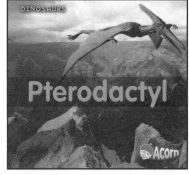

Hardback     978-0431184494

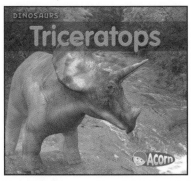

Hardback     978-0431184470

Hardback     978-0431184463

Hardback     978-0431184487

Find out about other titles from Heinemann Library on our website www.heinemann.co.uk/library